Welcome to our Mindfulness Mandala Coloring Book!

Be mindful during coloring.
Look at the mandalas, see the beautiful shapes
and color them with your favorite colors.
Breath slowly and be present.
Read the quotes from Buddha.

Have a wonderful time!

Visit our mindfulness shop at towerofmindfulness.com
to get your beautiful gold or rose gold coated
mindfulness reminder bracelet
that helps you be more mindful all the time.

Free Worldwide Shipping

"As you walk and eat and travel,
be where you are.
Otherwise you will miss most of your life."

"To conquer oneself
is a greater task
than conquering others."

"You cannot travel the path
until you have become the path itself."

"Set your heart on doing good.
Do it over and over again
and you will be filled with joy."

"Those who are free of resentful thoughts
surely find peace."

"No one saves us but ourselves.
No one can and no one may.
We ourselves must walk the path."

"What you think, you become.
What you feel, you attract.
What you imagine, you create."

"Your work is to discover your work
and then with all your heart
to give yourself to it."

"The secret of health for both mind and body
is not to mourn for the past, worry about the future,
or anticipate troubles, but to live
in the present moment wisely and earnestly."

"However many holy words you read,
however many you speak,
what good will they do you
if you do not act on upon them?"

"A generous heart, kind speech,
and a life of service and compassion
are the things which renew humanity."

"Purity or impurity depends on oneself.
No one can purify another."

"If we could see the miracle
of a single flower clearly,
our whole life would change."

"Believe nothing, no matter where you read it,
or who said it, no matter if I have said it,
unless it agrees with your own reason
and your own common sense."

"Three things cannot be long hidden:
the sun,
the moon,
and the truth."

"Wear your ego like a loose fitting garment."

"If you knew what I know about
the power of giving
you would not let a single meal pass
without sharing it in some way."

"Do not dwell in the past,
do not dream of the future,
concentrate the mind on the present moment."

"We are what we think.
All that we are arises with our thoughts.
With our thoughts, we make the world."

"In the sky, there is no distinction of east and west;
people create distinctions out of their own minds
and then believe them to be true."

"Health is the greatest gift,
contentment the greatest wealth,
faithfulness the best relationship."

"Happiness never decreases by being shared."

"There are only two mistakes
one can make along the road to truth:
not going all the way,
and not starting."

"You, yourself,
as much as anybody
in the entire universe,
deserve your love and affection."

"Your worst enemy cannot harm you as much
as your own unguarded thoughts."

"When the mind is pure,
joy follows like a shadow that never leaves."

"If you are quiet enough,
you will hear the flow of the universe.
You will feel its rhythm.
Go with this flow. Happiness lies ahead."

"All that we are is the result of
what we have thought.
The mind is everything.
What we think we become."

"The past is already gone,
the future is not yet here.
There's only one moment for you to live."

"Peace comes from within.
Do not seek it without."